.MY ROOM.

Poems to Annoy your Parents

chosen by Susie Gibbs

.KEEP.

OUT.

illustrated by
Jess Mikhail

OXFORD
UNIVERSITY PRESS

OXFORD
UNIVERSITY PRESS

Great Clarendon Street, Oxford OX2 6DP

Oxford University Press is a department of the University of Oxford.
It furthers the University's objective of excellence in research, scholarship,
and education by publishing worldwide in
Oxford New York
Auckland Bangkok Buenos Aires Cape Town Chennai
Dar es Salaam Delhi Hong Kong Istanbul Karachi Kolkata
Kuala Lumpur Madrid Melbourne Mexico City Mumbai Nairobi
São Paulo Shanghai Taipei Tokyo Toronto

This selection and arrangement copyright © Susie Gibbs 2003

Illustrations by Jess Mikhail 2003
Designed by Jo Samways

The moral rights of the author have been asserted

Database right Oxford University Press (maker)

First published 2003

British Library Cataloguing in Publication Data available

ISBN 0-19-276290-7

3 5 7 9 10 8 6 4 2

Typeset by Mary Tudge (Typesetting Services)

Printed in Great Britain by
Cox & Wyman Ltd, Reading, Berkshire

Contents

Swap? Sell? Small Ads Sell Fast!

1970 Dad. Good runner—needs one or
Two repairs—a few grey hairs but
Nothing a respray couldn't fix.
Would like a 1966 5-speed turbo
In exchange: something in the sporty
Twin-carb range.

1940s Granny. Not many like this
In such a clean and rust-free state.
You must stop by to view! All chrome
As new, original fascia retained
Upholstery unstained. Passed MOT
Last week: will only swap for some-
Thing quite unique.

Very low mileage brother. As eco-
Nomical as any other. Must mention
Does need some attention. Stream-
Lined, rear spoiler. Runs on milk,
Baby oil and gripe water. Serviced—
Needs rear wash/wipe. Only one
Owner—not yet run in. Will swap
For anything.

Trevor Millum

whoops!

I'm really really sorry
That I broke that dinner plate,
And spilled that sauce on the tablecloth,
And chipped that cup,
And dropped that glass on the floor.
Excuse me, did I hear you say
That I should please go out and play,
And not help clear the dishes any more?
I'm really really really sorry.
Sort of.

Judith Viorst

Mother's Nerves

My mother said, 'If just once more
I hear you slam that old screen door,
I'll tear out my hair! I'll dive in the stove!'
I gave it a bang and in she dove.

X. J. Kennedy

Top of the Pops?

My dad thinks he's a pop star.
His music's quite frenetic.
He waves his arms, rotates his hips,
I think he's just pathetic.

My dad goes on about success,
he's full of plans and schemes
to top the charts and tour the States,
but I say—in his dreams.

And when he goes to have a shower
Dad sings into the soap.
He's practising for his CD.
He hasn't got a hope.

My dad wails bits of Elvis
and says, 'How's that? Not bad!'
My mum thinks he's terrific,
but she is just as sad.

Dad wants to be discovered,
show that world that he's a whizz.
If only he'd discover
how embarrassing he is.

Alison Chisholm

If You Make Me Go To Bed Now

If you make me go to bed now
I am sure that I would hear
The sound of a mosquito
Buzzing loudly in my ear.
So, of course, I'd try to swat him
As I saw him try to land,
But I'd miss and break the bed lamp
And I know I'd hurt my hand,
So I'd need to find some bandages
To help to ease the pain,
But, in the dark, I'd bang my knee
So hard I'd need a cane,
And the ache would be so awful
That I wouldn't sleep a wink,
So I'd go to school next morning
And I couldn't even think,
So of course I'd fail my math test
And my other subjects, too,
I'd be so sad and embarrassed
There'd be nothing left to do
Except run away from home
About as far as I could go,
So I'd limp off to Alaska
And I'd trudge through ice and snow,
Till I met a hungry grizzly bear
All fierce and mean and mad
And as that grizzly ate me . . .

I'd remember Mom and Dad.
Yes, I'd think of my dear parents
And their final words to me,
'Get into bed this minute!
Turn that light off instantly!'

Let this poem be a warning
To all parents everywhere:
If you send your kids to bed,
They may be . . .
Digested by a bear.

Jeff Moss

My Mum (for Chris)

Calls it
Spaceman's Relish
And she
Zaps it
In a blender
Drowns it
In gravy
Mashes it
With potatoes
Hides it
Under chips
Scatters it
With sweetcorn
Nukes it
In the microwave
And follows it
With ice-cream:

But
It's
Still
Cabbage!

Kevin McCann

Food Mood

I'm out of broccoli,
Very luckily.
A carrot stick
Makes me sick.
I'm too fickle
To eat a pickle.
A dish with radish
Gets me madish.
I always balk
At a celery stalk.
Brussels sprouts
Are best thrown out.
And I like spinach
When it's finished.

Douglas Florian

Sick of Socks

Mum and Dad sent me to tidy my room
They gave me a duster, a mop, and a broom
They said to look under my bed and my chair
So I did – and I found stinky SOCKS everywhere.

They can tempt me with toffees or bribe me with chocs
But I'm not coming out till they've washed all my socks.

In wardrobes and cupboards, in corners and nooks
And shoved in my shoes and tucked into books
I found socks in their hundreds, socks by the score,
And they stank – so I threw them all out of the door.

They can tap-tap politely or hammer with knocks
But I'm not coming out till they've washed all my socks.

And now I am trapped in my room on my own
By the deadliest weapon the world's ever known:
An impassable smell bars my only way out
So unless someone saves me I'll starve, there's no
    doubt.

They can threaten to beat me, or pelt me with rocks
But I'm not coming out till they've washed all my socks.

And I haven't even started on the pants yet...

Liz Walker

Shocked!

Just look at you—
All studs and rings,
Those false nails
And that fake tattoo!
Your hair! My skirt!
Those boots! That hat!
No, Mum, you're NOT
Going out like that!

Sue Cowling

Divorce

I did not promise
to stay with you till death us do part, or
anything like that,
so part I must, and quickly. There are things
I cannot suffer
any longer: Mother, you have never, ever, said
a kind word
or a thank you for all the tedious chores I have done;
Father, your breath
smells like a camel's and gives me the hump;
all you ever say is:
'Are you off in the cream puff, Lady Muck?'
In this day and age?
I would be better off in an orphanage.

I want a divorce.
There are parents in the world whose faces turn
up to the light
who speak in the soft murmur of rivers
and never shout.
There are parents who stroke their children's cheeks
in the dead night
and sing in the colourful voices of rainbows,
red to blue.
These parents are not you. I never chose you.
You are rough and wild,
I don't want to be your child. All you do is shout
and that's not right.
I will file for divorce in the morning at first light.

Jackie Kay

Stomach Ache Supreme

If Mother asks you to make supper,
Don't protest, pout or scream.
You can use my favourite recipe
Called 'Stomach Ache Supreme'.

Get ice cream from the freezer,
Put it in a baking dish,
Pour some chocolate syrup on it
With a can of tuna fish.

Sprinkle it with chocolate chips,
Some salt and pepper too.
Dump a blob of honey on the top,
Now there's a 'treat' for you!

Spread peanut butter on it,
Add cinnamon to taste.
Garnish it with spinach
And a jar of almond paste.

Place it in the oven
And bake it for a while.
Then serve it to your family,
But don't forget to smile!

Give them heaping helpings,
Expect some stomach pain.
They'll never, never want you
To ever cook again!

Geraldine Nicholas

Parent-Free Zone

Parents please note
that from now on,
our room is a
'Parent-Free Zone'.

There will be no spying
under the pretence of
tidying up.

There will be no banning
of television programmes
because our room
is a tip.

No complaints about noise,
or remarks about the ceiling
caving in.

No disturbing the dirty
clothes
that have festered in piles
for weeks.

No removal of coffee cups
where green mould
has taken hold.
(These have been left there
for scientific research purposes.)

No reading of letters
to gain unauthorized information
which may be used against us
at a later date.

No searching through school bags
to discover if we've done our homework
or unearth forgotten notes.

Our room is a 'Parent-Free Zone'
and a notice is pinned to the door.

But just a minute,
there's something wrong . . .

MUM – WHY HAVEN'T YOU MADE OUR BEDS?

Brian Moses

Dish of the Day

Every time Dad cooks dinner
You have to make an enormous fuss
Encouraged by Mum
Who says that he won't do it again
unless you say it's the most wonderful,
  delicious, remarkable, fantastic, scrumptious,
  taste-bud popping, delectable feast,
You've ever clapped teeth on.
(*And* you have to volunteer for seconds.)
Whenever you swallow a mouthful
He hovers over you, asking:
'Is it all right—what do you think of it?
No really, tell me the truth!'

If you actually did tell him the truth,
that it's 'OK' or even 'Not bad',
He'd probably hit the roof
So instead you say:
'Wonderful, delicious, remarkable, fantastic,
  scrumptious, taste-bud popping . . .'
And he smiles.
A kind of proud but trying not to be big-headed
Smile and goes:
'Can't you think of anything else to say?'
Until your mate (who doesn't know how weird
  your dad is)
And who hasn't noticed your mum kicking him under
  the table and doing her goldfish face, which means:
'Keep your trap shut!'
Says:
'It's very nice, Mr Bishop. But it's only scrambled eggs.'

Lindsey Macrae

Peas

I eat my peas with honey,
I've done it all my life,
They do taste kind of funny,
But it keeps them on the knife.

Anon.

watch your French

When my mum tipped a panful of red-hot fat
Over her foot, she did quite a little chat,
And I won't tell you what she said
But it wasn't:
'Fancy that!
I must try in future to be far more careful
With this red-hot scalding fat!'

When my dad fell over and landed—splat!—
With a trayful of drinks (he'd tripped over the cat)
I won't tell you what he said
But it wasn't:
'Fancy that!
I must try in future to be far more careful
To step *round* our splendid cat!'

When Uncle Joe brought me a cowboy hat
Back from the States, the dog stomped it flat,
And I won't tell you what I said
But Mum and Dad yelled:
'STOP THAT!
Where did you learn that appalling language?
Come on. Where?'

'I've no idea,' I said,
'No idea.'

Kit Wright

when You Get Old

When you get old
And think you're sweet
Pull off your shoes
And smell your feet.

Anon.

It Makes Dad Mad

Let's ransack the toy box,
Cos it makes Dad mad.
Let's squeeze jelly in our socks,
Cos it makes Dad mad.
Let's wrestle in the flower beds,
And pour the compost on our heads;
Let's lock the dog in the garden shed,
Cos it makes Dad mad.

Let's spread toothpaste on the telly,
Cos it makes Dad mad.
Let's pour rhubarb in our wellies,
Cos it makes Dad mad.
Let's burst a bag of flour,
And put frogspawn in the shower;
Let's just scream for half an hour,
Cos it makes Dad mad.

Let's stamp in muddy puddles,
Cos it makes Dad mad.
Let's fill the bathroom up with bubbles,
Cos it makes Dad mad.
Let's tip treacle on the cat,
And chase it with a cricket bat;
Let's cut up the front door mat,
Cos it makes Dad mad.

Dad's asleep, don't wake him up.
The room's a mess, but we'll scrape it up.
He'll want some tea, so we'll make a cup.
Quiet—you can hear him snore,
He won't mind the sugar on the floor,
And all the milk spilt up the wall . . .
Watch the carpet—don't you fall!
What did you go and do that for?
COS IT MAKES DAD MAD!!

Dave Ward

From A Lesson for Mamma

Dear Mamma, if you just could be
A tiny little girl like me,
And I your mamma, you would see
    How nice I'd be to you.
I'd always let you have your way;
I'd never frown at you and say,
    'You are behaving ill today,
    Such conduct will not do.'

I'd buy you candy every day;
I'd go down town with you, and say,
'What would my darling like? You may
    Have anything you see.'
I'd never say, 'My pet, you know
'Tis bad for health and teeth, and so
I cannot let you have it. No—
    It would be wrong in me.'

I'd never say, 'Well, just a *few*!'
I'd let you stop your lessons too;
I'd say, 'They are too hard for you,
    Poor child, to understand.'
I'd put the books and slates away;
You shouldn't do a thing but play,
And have a party every day.
    Ah-h-h! wouldn't that be grand!

But, Mamma dear, you cannot grow
Into a little girl, you know,
And I can't be your mamma; so
    The only thing to do,
Is just for you to try and see
How very, very nice 'twould be
For *you* to do all this for *me*,
    Now, Mamma, *couldn't* you?

Sydney Dayre (Mrs Cochran)

Self-Sacrifice

Father, chancing to chastise
    His indignant daughter Sue,
Said, 'I hope you realize
    That this hurts me more than you.'

Susan straightway ceased to roar;
    'If that's really true,' said she,
'I can stand a good deal more;
    Pray go on, and don't mind me.'

Harry Graham

Another Bad Day for Mum

Mum! Mum!
They've sent me home from school today.
They say I'm troublesome.

Mum! Mu-u-um!
How do you mend these ornaments?
Putting them there was dumb.

Mum! MUUUUUUM!
The grumpy next-door-neighbour's here,
The one you said was scum.

Mum! Mum!
The brand new sofa's all messed up
With bits of chewing gum.

Mum! Mu-u-um!
The dog's been at my birthday cake.
He hasn't left a crumb.

Mum! MUUUUUUM!
The babysitter and me've been sick.
We're sorry we drank your rum.

Nick Toczek

The Sponge

The sponge is not, as you suppose,
    A funny kind of weed;
He lives below the deep blue sea,
An animal, like you and me,
    Though not so good a breed.

And when the sponges go to sleep
    The fearless diver dives;
He prongs them with a cruel prong,
And, what I think is rather wrong,
    He also prongs their wives.

For I expect they love them well,
    And sing them little songs,
And though, of course, they have no heart,
It hurts them when they're forced to part—
    Especially with prongs.

I know you'd rather not believe
    Such dreadful things are done;
Alas, alas, it is the case;
And every time you wash your face
    You use a skeleton.

While that round hole in which you put
    Your finger and your thumb,
And tear the nice new sponge in two,
As I have told you *not* to do,
    Was once his osculum.

So that is why I seldom wash,
    However black I am,
Or use my flannel if I must,
Though even that, to be quite just,
    Was once a little lamb.

A. P. Herbert

The National Union of Children

NUC has just passed a weighty resolution:
'Unless all parents raise our rate of pay
This action will be taken by our members
(The resolution comes in force today):—

'Noses will not be blown (sniffs are in order),
Bedtime will get preposterously late,
Ice-cream and crisps will be consumed for breakfast,
Unwanted cabbage left upon the plate,

'Earholes and fingernails can't be inspected,
Overtime (known as homework) won't be worked,
Reports from school will all say 'Could do better',
Putting bricks back in boxes may be shirked.'

Roy Fuller

The National Association of Parents

Of course, NAP's answer quickly was forthcoming
(It was a matter of emergency),
It issued to the Press the following statement
(Its Secretary appeared upon TV):—

'True that the so-called Saturday allowance
Hasn't kept pace with prices in the shops,
But neither have, alas, parental wages:
NUC's claim would ruin kind, hard-working Pops.

'Therefore, unless that claim is now abandoned,
Strike action for us, too, is what remains;
In planning for the which we are in process
Of issuing, to all our members, canes.'

Roy Fuller

My Phobias

Fear of water:
When did that face last see a flannel?
Those mucky fingers last see soap?

Fear of straight lines:
Why don't you use a ruler?
When did that hair last see a comb?

Fear of green things:
That cabbage is good for you!
Come and help me weed the garden!

Fear of neatness:
Your bedroom! No wonder
You can't find a thing!

Fear of animals:
The dog needs a run!
Can you feed the budgie for me?

Fear of being upright:
Come on, get up, you lazy-bones!
Are you going to lie on that couch all night!

My mum and dad think
I've got half the phobias in the universe.
I let them think I'm *deaf*!

Which, of course, is not the same as being daft!

Matt Simpson

Next Please!

Please could I have an ice-cream?

Hazelnut, pistachio,
rum and raisin, strawberry dream?
Chocolate mint or chocolate chip,
toffee walnut, coffee cream?
Orange with vanilla,
raspberry ripple, blackberry flip?
Mango, lime or lemon,
coconut or cherry dip?
Apple, almond, chestnut,
apricot, banana, cheese . . . ?

> *THANKS!*
> *I think I'll have a lolly . . .*
> > > *please!*

Judith Nicholls

Wasp in the Kitchen

Wasp in the kitchen, going mad!
Wasp in the kitchen, Dad! Dad! Dad!
Wasp in the dinner, run, run, run!
Wasp in the gravy, Mum! Mum! Mum!

Big brave father, here he comes:
    'Wasps won't hurt you
    wasps are chums
    wasps are gentle
    wasps are fun
    pretty jackets
    pretty tums . . .'
On Dad's finger,
on Dad's palm,
wasps are friendly,
wasps don't harm.
On Dad's wrist,
on Dad's cuff.
My dad's clever.
My dad's tough.
On his elbow,
glasses,
clothes.
On his chin
and
    UP HIS NOSE!

FATHER'S YELLING!!
See him run!
Help, help, help!
Mum! Mum! Mum!

Peter Dixon

My Best Pal

There's a boy in our class
Name of Billy McMillan,
And everyone knows
He's a bit of a villain.

My mum doesn't like him,
No more does my dad,
They say he's a hooligan;
This makes me mad.

Okay, so he's scruffy
And hopeless at school,
But that doesn't mean he's
An absolute fool.
He's brilliant at spitting
And juggling with balls,
And no one can beat him
At peeing up walls.

He's my best mate
And I think he's just fine,
You can choose your friends,
And I will choose mine.

Colin McNaughton

Thank You, Dad, For Everything

Thank you for laying the carpet, Dad,
Thank you for showing us how,
But what is that lump in the middle, Dad?
And why is it saying mia-ow?

Doug MacLeod

No

No. I refuse to.
No. I don't choose to.
No. I most certainly don't.
You've made a mistake
If you thought you could make
Me. No no no—I won't.

No. You could beat me.
No. You could eat me
Up from my head to my toes,
And inside your belly,
Loudly and yelly,
I'd keep saying no's.

No. You could sock me,
Feed me some broccoli,
Tickle me till I turned blue,
But in between giggles
And sniggles and wriggles
I'd say no to you.

No No No No No No No No No

No. You could tease me,
Please, pretty please, me,
Cry till your eyes washed away.
You could beg till you're old,
But I'd look at you cold.
En-oh is what I'd say.

No. You could shove me.
No. You could love me
With kisses all squishy and wet.
You could scratch me with claws
But I'd say no, because
. . . because . . . because . . .
I forget!

Judith Viorst

urgent Note To My Parents

Don't ask me to do what I can't do
Only ask me to do what I can
Don't ask me to be what I can't be
Only ask me to be what I am

Don't one minute say 'Be a big girl'
And the next, 'You're too little for that'
PLEASE don't ask me to be where I can't be
PLEASE be happy with right where I'm at.

Hiawyn Oram

Think of Eight Numbers

Think of eight numbers from one to nine—
That's fine.
Now pick up the phone and dial them all—
That's making a call.
Now wait till somebody answers,
Then shout 'Yickety-yick!' and hang up quick,
And sit for awhile,
And have a smile,
And start all over again.

Shelley Silverstein

Daddy Fell into the Pond

Everyone grumbled. The sky was grey.
We had nothing to do and nothing to say.
We were nearing the end of a dismal day.
And there seemed to be nothing beyond,
   Then
      Daddy fell into the pond!

And everyone's face grew merry and bright,
And Timothy danced for sheer delight.
'Give me the camera, quick, oh quick!
He's crawling out of the duckweed!' Click!

Then the gardener suddenly slapped his knee,
And doubled up, shaking silently,
And the ducks all quacked as if they were daft,
And it sounded as if the old drake laughed.
Oh, there wasn't a thing that didn't respond
   When
      Daddy fell into the pond!

Alfred Noyes

CLick....

Little Treasure

You don't understand.
You don't understand.
You won't let me play
In a rock and roll band.

You don't understand.
You don't understand.
I want to wear rings
On each foot and each hand.

You don't understand.
You don't understand.
Tell me. Why can't I bury
The dog in the sand?

It just isn't fair.
It just isn't fair.
Why can't I swim in the sea
When I'm bare?

It just isn't fair.
It just isn't fair.
Tell me. Why won't you let me
Dreadlock my hair?

It just isn't fair.
It just isn't fair.
Why do my brother
And I have to share?

It just isn't fair.
It just isn't fair.
Why can't I have
Those new trainers to wear?

It just isn't fair.
It just isn't fair.
Nobody loves me.
Why does nobody care?

John Kitching

The Sight of Parents Kissing is Very well worth Missing

Do you have to do that?
You're not teenagers after all.
You're blocking up the hall
or else sprawled
on the sofa.
Frankly I don't think it's on
for people with three children
to go on kissing for so long.
It's wrong!
And you look nothing like
a pair of fluffy bunnies to me.
She might be your 'sweety-darling'
but she's also 'Mum'.
Put her down please!
We know where she's been
—hoovering under the beds
and unblocking the loo—
How can you still fancy someone
who
does the kind of stuff that she has to do?
You've made her all red in the face
and she's made you
all gooey-eyed.
Parents shouldn't act like this
in fact no one should
who's over twenty-two.

Lindsey Macrae

when My Friend Bob Came to Stay

My friend Bob
On day one
Threw a stinkbomb just for fun
With a knick-knack paddy-whack
It's not what he meant
But his bed is where it went.

My friend Bob
On day two
Flushed our hamster down the loo
With a knick-knack paddy-whack
Hamster wasn't dumb
That night it bit him on the bum.

My friend Bob
On day three
Tied my parents to a tree
With a knick-knack paddy-whack
Hungry as can be
He let them go to make his tea.

My friend Bob
On day four
Said that he was going to war
With a knick-knack paddy-whack
Order was restored
When he fell on to his sword.

My friend Bob
On day five
Took my dad's car for a drive
With a knick-knack paddy-whack
Terrible mistake –
Found he couldn't reach the brake.

My friend Bob
On day six
Said that he would stop his tricks
With a knick-knack paddy-whack
He'd be mild and he'd be meek
So could he come again next week?

Liz Walker

Story Time

Sorry Dad, but
As soon as you start
Telling your stories
I really want to go to sleep.

I'm sure
They're really interesting stories
About how you nearly . . .
Sorry Dad, nodded off there a minute.

Right, I'm awake now.
Tell me about how you nearly
Played for England.
Gosh, I'm tired.

I think I'll go to bed soon.
Sorry Dad, but
Were you saying something?
One of your interesting stories?

Ian McMillan

IRON MAN

Proud on his board,
Surf wise and brave
There goes my father
Riding a wave.
A flurry of legs,
The sea in a lather,
And there goes the wave,
Riding my father.

Max Fatchen

Dear Mum,

while you were out
a cup went and broke itself,
a crack appeared in the blue vase
your great-great-grandad
brought back from Mr Ming in China.
Somehow, without me even turning on the tap,
the sink mysteriously overflowed.
A strange jam-stain,
about the size of a boy's hand,
appeared on the kitchen wall.
I don't think we will ever discover
exactly how the cat
managed to turn on the washing-machine
(specially from the inside),
or how Sis's pet rabbit went and mistook
the waste-disposal unit for a burrow.
I can tell you I was scared when,
as if by magic,
a series of muddy footprints
appeared on the new white carpet.
I was being good
(honest)
but I think the house is haunted so,
knowing you're going to have a fit,
I've gone over to Gran's for a bit.

Brian Patten

There was a young lady...

There was a young lady of Tottenham,
Who's no manners or else she's forgotten 'em.
At tea at the vicar's,
She tore off her knickers,
Because, she explained, she felt 'ot in 'em.

Anon.

A buxom young lady...

A buxom young lady of Bude
Remarked, 'Men are exceedingly rude;
When I bathe in the sea
They all follow me
To see if my bosoms protrude.'

Anon.

The Tiger

The Tiger on the other hand, is kittenish and mild,
He makes a pretty playfellow for any little child;
And mothers of large families (who claim to
  common sense)
Will find a Tiger well repays the trouble and
  expense.

Hilaire Belloc

You little monkey!

My mum said
I was behaving
like a little monkey.

So I climbed
on to the sofa
and started swinging
on the door.

When she told me to stop,
I made chattering noises
and pretended
to scratch my armpits.

I refused
to talk properly
until tea-time,
when all I got
was a plate of nuts
and a banana!

So I decided
to stop
monkeying about.

John Foster

Sometimes Even Parents Win

There was a young lady from Gloucester
Who complained that her parents both bossed her,
So she ran off to Maine.
Did her parents complain?
Not at all—they were glad to have lost her.

John Ciardi

Acknowledgements

We are grateful for permission to reproduce the following poems:

Hilaire Belloc: 'The Tiger' from *The Bad Child's Book of Beasts* (Duckworth, 1923), copyright © Hilaire Belloc 1923, reprinted by permission of PFD on behalf of The Estate of Hilaire Belloc.

Sue Cowling: 'Shocked!' first published in *Unzip Your Lips Again* edited by Paul Cookson (Macmillan, 1999), reprinted by permission of the author.

Max Fatchen: 'Iron Man' from *A Paddock of Poems* (Penguin Australia, 1987), reprinted by permission of John Johnson (Authors' Agent) Limited.

John Foster: 'You Little Monkey' from *You Little Monkey* (Oxford University Press, 1996), reprinted by permission of the author.

Douglas Florian: 'Food Mood' from *Bing Bang Boing* (Harcourt, 1994), copyright © 1994 by Douglas Florian, reprinted by permission of Harcourt Inc.

Roy Fuller: 'The Nat'l Union of Children' and 'The Nat'l Association of Parents' both from *The World Through the Window* (Blackie, 1989), reprinted by permission of John Fuller.

Harry Graham: 'Self Sacrifice' from *Ruthless Rhymes For Heartless Homes* (Edward Arnold, 1909), reprinted by permission of Laura Dance.

A.P. Herbert: 'The Sponge' from *Wisdom For The Wise* (Methuen & Co. Ltd, 1930), reprinted by permission of A. P. Watt Ltd on behalf of Jocelyn Hale and Teresa Elizabeth Perkins.

X.J. Kennedy: 'Mother's Nerves' from *One Winter Night in August* (Atheneum, 1975), copyright © X. J. Kennedy 1975, reprinted by permission of Curtis Brown Ltd, New York.

Doug MacLeod: 'Thank You, Dad, For Everything' from *The Fed Up Family Album* (Penguin Australia, 1983), reprinted by permission of the publisher.

Lindsey Macrae: 'Dish of the Day' and 'The Sight of Parents Kissing is Very Well Worth Missing' both from *How To Avoid Kissing Your Parents In Public* (Puffin, 2000) copyright © Lindsey Macrae 2000, reprinted by permission of Penguin Books Ltd.

Colin McNaughton: 'My Best Pal' from *There's An Awful Lot of Weirdos in Our Neighbourhood* (Walker Books, 1987) copyright © Colin McNaughton 1987, reprinted by permission of Walker Books Limited, London.

Brian Moses: 'Parent-Free Zone' from *Don't Look At Me In That Tone of Voice!* (Macmillan, 1998) copyright © Brian Moses 1998, reprinted by permission of the author.

Alfred Noyes: 'Daddy Fell into the Pond' from *Collected Poems* (John Murray Publishers, 1950), reprinted by permission of The Society of Authors as the Literary Representative of the Estate of Alfred Noyes.